A FRESH LOOK
AT THE
NEW TESTAMENT
DEACON

WORKBOOK

BY DR. JOHN H. WALKER, D.MIN.

A FRESH LOOK AT THE NEW TESTAMENT DEACON

WORKBOOK

BY DR. JOHN H. WALKER, D.MIN.

A Fresh Look at the New Testament Deacon Workbook
Copyright © 2001 Orman Press
Lithonia, GA

ISBN: 1-891773-15-1

Printed in the United States of America

TABLE OF CONTENTS

COURSE PURPOSE AND OBJECTIVE

The primary purpose and objective of this course is to come to a clearer understanding of the role, responsibility and work of deacons. A secondary objective is to gain knowledge, information and understanding to equip deacons to perform their task effectively and efficiently, and to share in the fellowship of servant-hood as they labor for our Lord and Savior Jesus Christ.

INTRODUCTION

In the Baptist Churches, the deacon suffers from a lack of pre-ministry training. There are many persons selected to serve in the diaconate, because of a lack of able bodies. These persons generally have good intentions for the work at hand, yet they lack informative preparation. Consequently, after a period of time, they may view themselves as being vanguards of the spiritual welfare of the church. Their sense of service changes to a sense of privileged authority. The lack of preparation sends the deacon away asking, "What is my role in this church?"

For many pastors there is a constant conflict with the diaconate over power and authority. This conflict issue occurs because persons operating in this office have not been adequately prepared for Christian service. In some churches, those chosen for the diaconate are instructed on how to take orders and respect the order-giver. The order-giver might be the pastor or the chairperson of the deacon's ministry. This person can sometimes want only their "personal agenda" to be top priority. As a result, conflict arises from clashing personalities with different definitions of the same idea.

This is a training guide for deacons. It is not a "complete" or final word on the preparation process, but it is a tool to help those preparing to do the work of a deacon.

PRINCIPLES OF CHRISTIAN LEADERSHIP

There is always a great need for qualified laypersons to serve in leadership roles. However, before believers seek such avenues, they should explore these principles:

1. Faithfulness is the chief qualification for leadership.
2. Leaders will be held to higher standards than non-leaders.
3. Leaders lead by example.
4. Spiritual leaders inspire cooperation from the heart.

FACTS ABOUT THE CHURCH

1. Establishment   Matthew 16:18
2. Authority   Matthew 16:19-20
3. Leadership   Jeremiah 3:15

                             Numbers 12:6

                             Numbers 16:28

SERVANTS OF CHRIST

Christian service provides equal opportunities for all those who believe in and follow Jesus Christ. The Bible teaches there are many opportunities for all believers to serve God (Romans 12:4-8; 1 Corinthians 12:4-11). The Holy Spirit of God provides these opportunities. The gifts of God are intended to do the following: (1) encourage the body of Christ to share these gifts with all humankind and (2) develop a strong institutional body of believers whose bond is not easily broken (Ephesians 4:7-16).

The focus of this manual centers on the ministry of the deacon. These persons are a selected--not a privileged--group chosen to assist in the pastoral care of the church. The title roles come from the Greek word "diakonos." This word is both meaningful and colorful. Diakonos means "servant," as rendering free service. The work carries a colorful message: one who goes through the dirt for their master--one who serves others on the behalf of another.

Diakonos are not subject to one sex.[1] The list of qualifications in 1 Timothy 3:11 requires that "women" must "likewise" be similar in character to the men. Although this remark may refer to the wives of male deacons, it probably should be interpreted as a parenthetical reference to female deacons, or deaconess. Romans 16:1 refers to Phoebe as a diakonos of the church at Cenchrea.

The deaconess is mentioned prominently in early A.D. Christian writings. They cared for needy fellow believers, visited the sick, and were especially charged with assisting in the baptism of women converts.

The whole idea of serving is a considerable honor for those chosen to serve. The major idea of diakonos is "one who helps." It is not to be confused with the word doulos, which means "slave" or "bondservant." Doulos refers to the servant ordained by God, while diakonos refers to the servant called by the church.

In the Bible, Christ lifted service to an entirely new and exciting level. To Him service was greatness, and He exemplified this in His earthly life. An essential New Testament passage is Mark 10:45. In this passage, Christ indicated He came not to be served, but to serve and sacrifice Himself as a ransom for humankind. We should have the same attitude as we serve others.

JESUS' TEACHINGS ON CHRISTIAN LEADERSHIP
(A SERVANT'S MODEL)

PERSONAL REVIEW

Prayerfully take time to consider your answers
to the following questions.[2]

1. Am I seen as a servant and therefore trusted as a leader?

    ___Yes   ___No

2. Am I willing to wait on the invitation of the Host to sit at the head table?

    ___Yes   ___No

3. Do people see the humility of Christ in my life?

    ___Yes   ___No

4. Is Jesus genuinely Master of my life?

    ___Yes   ___No

5. Am I willing to humble myself like Jesus in order to allow God to accomplish His plan for my life?

___Yes   ___No

A. THE SEVEN PRINCIPLES OF SERVANT LEADERSHIP

1. Servant leaders humble themselves and wait for God to exalt them. (Luke 14:7-11)
2. Servant leaders follow Jesus rather than positions. (Mark 10:32-40)
3. Servant leaders give up personal rights to find greatness in service to others. (Mark 10:41-45)
4. Servant leaders can risk serving others because they trust that God is in control of their lives. (John 13:3)
5. Servant leaders take up Jesus' towel of servanthood to meet the needs of others. (John 13:4-11)
6. Servant leaders share their responsibility and authority with others to meet a greater need. (Acts 6:1-6)
7. Servant leaders multiply their leadership by empowering others to lead. (Exodus 18:17-23)

B. YOU AS A SERVANT LEADER

Jesus said that the way the world practices leadership would not be the pattern among His true discipleship. (Mark 10:43)

C. JESUS, THE SERVANT LEADER

Servants and slaves do not define leadership in the world's dictionary.

Jesus is our only true model of servant leadership.

DEACON'S PLEDGE

We pledge ourselves as duly elected deacons

of the Baptist Church. Our firm commitment is to work toward the

attainment of excellence in the fulfillment of our assigned ministry.

We see ourselves as servants of Jesus Christ and lay assistants to

the pastor. Our efforts will be for the general welfare and spiritual

well-being of our respected church families. We promise to never

become a hindrance to the pastor or to see ourselves as his

superior; we are chosen to pray for him and with him,

and to be deacons who uphold the pastor's arms.

LESSON I

UNDERSTANDING THE ROLE & RESPONSIBILITIES OF THE PASTOR

WHO IS THE PASTOR?

The main obstacle in the inability of deacons to minister to the pastor is that they do not understand the role and responsibilities of the pastor. Deacons many times do not have their vision of God's kingdom evaluated beyond the laity (laos). They often think too much like laity, as opposed to spiritual leaders.[3] Thus, their vision of the pastor is oftentimes shaped by tradition or by their relationship with the pastor prior to becoming a leader. There are two traditional concepts that must be overcome: The <u>first</u> is that the pastor is someone who is only interested in money. Deacons must recognize that church money does not belong to a church officer or to an official church group. It is first the Lord's and then the congregations, to distribute under the leadership of the Holy Spirit. It is indeed easy for young men and women to get a sense of proprietorship about money. However, the tithe brought to the church ceases to belong to the one who brings it.

The <u>second</u> traditional concept is that the pastor is someone who is to preach only, and anything the pastor does outside of preaching is non-spiritual. This type of attitude fosters contention, causing both sides to closely watch each other. However, the Biblical model of who the pastor is, is a shepherd that <u>pursues</u>, <u>protects</u> and <u>provides</u> for the sheep. Therefore, it becomes vitally important for deacons to minister to their pastor in order to reduce the stress and spiritual strain upon him.

TRADITIONAL MINDSET

a.

b.

BIBLICAL MODEL

a.

b.

c.

SPIRITUAL RELATIONSHIP

a.

b.

c.

SPIRITUAL MODEL

- Exodus 18:13-22

- Jeremiah 3:15

- Jeremiah 23:4

ROLE AND RESPONSIBILITY OF THE PASTOR

The pastor is the spiritual and administrative head of the church. As spiritual leader, he is to teach and preach the Gospel and provide leadership in developing the various ministries necessary, as God directs him. The pastor's role and responsibility can be clearly defined by the example Jesus set in Matthew 4:23 and the seven shepherd models given by Dr. Benjamin S. Baker in his book *Shepherding the Sheep*.

A. THE FOUR PASTORAL MODELS--MATTHEW 4:23

1. _____

2. _____

3. _____

4. _____

B. THE SEVEN SHEPHERD MODELS

1. Shepherd

2. Overseer - (Acts 20:28)

3. Supervisor - (Matthew 10:1, 7-8)

4. Organizer - (Exodus 18:17-23)

5. Enabler - (Ephesians 4:11-12)

6. Administrator - (1 Corinthians 9:19, 22)

7. Counselor - (Isaiah 1:18)

DEACONS MUST UNDERSTAND THE PASTOR'S MINISTRY

- 1 Peter 5:2
- Mark 10:45
- Philippians 2:6-8

DEACONS MUST UNDERSTAND THE PASTOR'S HUMAN LIMITATIONS

- John 1:6-9

- 1 Corinthians 1:26-29

- 1 Corinthians 9:26-27

DEACONS MUST UNDERSTAND THE PASTOR'S DIVINE AUTHORITY

- John 1:6-8

- Romans 10:14-15

- 1 Samuel 26:7-11

DEACONS MUST UNDERSTAND THE HEAVENLY COMMISSION

- Acts 6:1

- Acts 6:2

- Acts 6:3-4

LESSON II

THE ROLE AND RESPONSIBILITIES OF DEACONS

WHAT IS A DEACON?

The term diakonos (deacon) denotes service, ministration, helper or bondservant, one who has sold himself, by choice, for service. His ministry is non-preaching; but he should be apt to teach. There are proven men and women in the faith who will serve as right-hand men to the pastor in secular and business matters of the church, such as conducting worship services and assisting in carrying out the ordinances of the church. They should be knowledgeable of the doctrine of the Baptist Church.

The leadership of the Holy Spirit gave rise to the office of deacon in the New Testament churches. Divine wisdom brought deacons into being. The role of the diakonos is not relegated to men only. The list of qualifications in 1 Timothy 3:11 requires that "women" must likewise be similar in character to the men. Although this remark may refer to the wives of male deacons, it probably should be interpreted as a parenthetical reference to female deacons, or deaconesses. Romans 16:1 refers to Phebe as a diakonos of the church at Cenchrea.

The seven men in Acts 6 are not called deacons. They are most often referred to as the seven. It is a matter of general agreement, however, that the election of these seven qualified men can be found in 1 Timothy 3:8-12. The qualifications of the men who served as deacons are carefully outlined in the introduction of Paul's epistle to church at Philippi: "Paul and Timothy, the servants of Jesus Christ, to all the saints in Christ Jesus, which are at Philippi, with the bishops and deacons" (Philippians 1:1). Beginning in the Jerusalem church, the office of the deacon had developed with the approval and blessing of the Holy Spirit. A distinction must be drawn between the work that a deacon does and the office that he holds.

WHY ARE DEACONS NEEDED?

The question is, "Are deacons needed now?" Deacons are needed in churches today just as much as they were needed in the first church at Jerusalem.

1. **Based on the New Testament**--Acts 6:2-4, "And the twelve summoned the congregation of the disciples and said, it is not desirable for us to neglect the word of God in order to serve tables, but select from among you, brethren, seven men of good reputation, full of the spirit and of wisdom, who we may put in charge of this task. However, we will devote ourselves to prayer and to the ministry of the word."

2. **Office misunderstood**--to assist not as a board of directors, but to minister as servants.

3. **To free the minister**--not free from, but free to.

4. **To be a promoter of church harmony.**

5. **To support the welfare of the membership.**

6. **To be more effective witnesses** - Acts 6:7, "And the word of God kept on spreading, and the number of the disciples multiplied in Jerusalem greatly; and a great company of the priests were becoming obedient to the faith."

ROLE OF THE DEACONS

Deacons, as well as pastors, must be reminded that their positions are ones of service. The biblical example always shows that both are to be accountable. Deacons should remember that God has chosen them to lead His church through the pastoral office. Therefore, deacons must understand that their role is not one of ruling the pastor, but seeking to hear God's spirit speaking to them when the pastor attempts to lead. The church operates through Christ and not through deacons. The question of deacons' authority should also remind us that in the early church, there was no chairman; all deacons were of equal footing. The word chairman implies authority that one holds, which is not true in the case of the deacon's ministry. Many churches have been destroyed by a chairman of a deacon board that exercised power that was not his. Like all other deacons, the chairman has only <u>one vote</u>. It is very important that the chairman of the deacons does not exercise his will over the pastor or the congregation.

The deacons are responsible primarily for three functions in the church, which are all related to a position of service.

1. The Lord's Table

The deacon is to administer Holy Communion as instructed by the pastor. The deacon is to make sure that all things are in order in relation to worship--making sure the table has been properly supplied by the deaconesses and helping to maintain a sense of order and worship during this service. The deacons should see to it that those who wish to have Holy Communion are served in their homes or at the hospital, whatever the case may be.

2. The Table of the Poor

The deacons should report those in need (i.e., those unable to obtain the bare necessities of life) to the fellowship and make sure they are taken care of to the best ability of the church. Deacons must remember that when the Bible speaks of the poor, it refers to those without family or other resources beyond the church. Thus deacons must be mission minded. It is a good idea to have deacons as part of the missionary circle to help the circle maintain its direction.

3. The Table of the Pastor

The deacon, as a church leader, should be in the forefront encouraging the church to support the pastor so that he may do ministry. The deacon should not allow members to use the salary of the pastor as a means of creating confusion and implementing control. The deacon, as next in the line of authority of biblical office, will be held accountable by God in this matter. They are to make sure that the pastor does not suffer or go lacking because of the sacrifices he makes. Deacons should make sure that those who make financial decisions about the church are spiritually minded and understand the biblical examples of how money is to be used.

PARADIGMS FOR LEADERSHIP

I have chosen to talk about the <u>qualification</u> and <u>responsibilities</u> of deacons under three paradigms:

BEING	*BECOMING*	*DOING*
Christ the Savior	Christ the Teacher	Christ the Servant
Theo-centric	Christ-centric	Pneumo-centric
Upward	Inward	Outward
Heart	Head	Hand
Worship	Nurture	Outreach
Know	Feel	Do
Cognitive	Affective	Vocational
Identify Gifts	Accept Gifts	Utilize Gifts
I-Thou	I-We	I-You [4]

THE DEACON AND HIS CALLING

The origin and work of the deacon is rooted in at least five theological presuppositions.

1.
2.

3.

4.

5.

A person does not become a deacon just for the honor. The deacon is set apart to serve. He is committed to serve God and his fellow man. **The office of deacon is not one of authority, but one of service**. The original purpose for the establishment of deacon service was to preserve the spiritual fellowship of the church.

The deacon's function is that of an assistant to the pastor. He is chosen by the church, at the suggestion of the pastor, to do a threefold task as needs occur:

1.

2.

3.

THE DEACON'S RELATIONSHIP TO THE CHURCH

The deacon and pastor comprise a team that should be most intimately connected and thoroughly cooperative in the work of the Lord and the service of the church. The necessary characteristics of a man who is selected to serve as a deacon are:

1.

2.

3.

4.

5.

6.

THE DEACON--PARTNER WITH HIS PASTOR

1 Corinthians 3:10

PASTORS AND DEACONS SHARE SIMILAR QUALIFICATIONS

1 Timothy 3:1

DIFFERENCES IN THE PASTOR'S AND DEACON'S LEADERSHIP ROLES

The church calls the pastor to be a generalist leader. In his leadership role, the pastor serves as a player-coach-enabler. He develops people. As generalist leader, the pastor leads the church to determine its spiritual mission.

Deacons are exemplary leaders. They serve as models for fellow Christians to follow. As exemplary leaders, deacons often serve behind the scene--out of the spotlight or central focus of activities. Some guidelines for deacons are as follow:

- **Understand the Pastor and His Work**
- **Pray for the Pastor**
- **Affirm the Pastor**
- **Support the Pastor**
- **Enjoy Fellowship with the Pastor**

THE DEACON'S MINISTRY

The deacon seeks not his own will, but to know and do the will of Christ and the church he serves.

The deacons help the pastor by:

1.

2.

3.

4.

5.

The deacons help the church by:

1.

2.

3.

4.

5.

6.

THE DEACON TRANSLATES HIS QUALIFICATIONS INTO SERVICE

God, in His Divine wisdom, set the qualifications for a deacon high because the work of the deacon is spiritual in nature:

- **A Man of Honest Report** (Acts 6:13)
- **Full of the Holy Spirit** (Acts 6:3)
- **Full of Wisdom** (Acts 6:5)
- **Full of Faith** (Acts 6:5)
- **Grave** (1 Timothy 3:8)
- **Not Double-Tongued** (1 Timothy 3:8)
- **Not Given to Much Wine** (1 Timothy 3:8)
- **Not Greedy of Filthy Lucre** (1 Timothy 3:8)
- **A Holder of the Faith** (1 Timothy 3:9)
- **Tested and Proven**(1 Timothy 3:10)
- **Blameless** (1 Timothy 3:10)
- **Christian Family Life** (1 Timothy 3:11-12)
- **Husband of One Wife** (1 Timothy 3:12)
- **Rules His Children and His Own House Well** (1 Timothy 3:12)
- **Bold in Faith** (1 Timothy 3:13)

The prayer of the deacon should well be the same as St. Augustine's, who once prayed, *"O Lord, grant that I may do thy will as if it were my will; so that I mayest do my will as if it were thy will."*[5]

The deacon's task concerning spiritual gifts (1 Corinthians 12)

1.

2.

3.

LESSON III

THE WORK OF THE DEACON

The work of the deacon should be a joyful response to his spiritual relationship with God. The New Testament deacon had a work to do concerning the membership of the church. The original seven men were in fact concerned with personal relations in the church.

DEACONS AND THE WORSHIP SERVICES

The deacons should come to the sanctuary together to lead the devotional service.[6] They are not to coincidentally "pop in." They should have arranged beforehand who will sing and lead prayer. If they are going to invite the congregation to pray, sing or testify, they should make this known at the start of the devotional service. Scripture selections, responsive readings, songs, testimonies and so on, should be prepared in advance and delivered in an orderly fashion. The deacons should know who will help in receiving the offering, who will pray and who will help during the invitation.

A. Participants

1. Pastor

2. Associate Ministers

3. Deacons

4. Minister of Music

5. Ushers

B. Deacon's Positions

1. Within the pastor's eye view (pulpit)

2. Alert to pulpit, Bible, seating and other aides

3. Offering table

4. Usher assistance

5. Physical comfort--too hot, too cold, doors, windows, noise

6. Pastor's doorkeepers

DEACONS LEADING IN WORSHIP

1. Responsibilities

A. Devotional Period

B. Offering (offertory appeal prayer)

C. Preaching service

D. Invitation

E. Pastor's watchman

2. Services Rendered

A. Pray

B. Sing

C. Encourage

D. Lead Testimonial Service

E. Keep Order

F. Assist Pastor

DEACONS AND CHURCH ADMINISTRATION

A. Ministry Model

B. Membership

    1.

    2.

    3.

    4.

C. Money

D. Mission/Benevolence

E. Baptism--Colossians 2:12

    1.

    2.

    3.

    4.

    5.

    6.

    7.

F. Lord's Supper--1 Corinthians 11:24-34

1.

2.

3.

4.

5.

DEACONS CARRYING OUT A MOTION FOR NEW MEMBERS

Motions are always begun with the phrase "I move," and you must state what action you wish to initiate after someone says, "I move."[7] ("I so move" is a commonly used phrase, but an improper motion, especially when nothing follows this statement indicating what motion you are suggesting be accepted.) Listed below are examples of proper "motions" for accepting new members into the church:

1. Candidate for Baptism

After listening to the report of the Clerk, I move that (brother) (sister) (name) be accepted as a candidate for baptism.[8] After baptism, and upon receiving the right hand of fellowship, (he) (she) will be granted all rights, privileges and responsibilities of the church.

2. Christian Experience

After listening to the report of the Clerk, I move that (brother) (sister) (name) be accepted as a member of the said Church, and after receiving the right hand of fellowship, be granted all rights, privileges and responsibilities of this church.

OR

After listening to the report of the Clerk, I move that (brother) (sister) (name) be accepted as a member of said Church pending the receipt of (his) (her) letter from (church name), and upon receiving of the right hand of fellowship, be granted all rights, privileges and responsibilities of this church.

DEACON'S ROLE IN EVANGELISM

It is important that deacons be trained in, or knowledgeable of, how to lead others to Christ. One of the mission goals of the church is to evangelize; therefore, we must know how to biblically lead others to Christ.

1.

2.

3.

Obstacles that get in the way of deacons being effective witnesses.[9]

1.

2.

3.

THINGS THAT HELP DEACONS IN EVANGELISM

1.

2.

DEACONS AND VISITATION

A. Understanding the "Why" of Visitation

Kinds of Visitations

   a.

   b.

   c.

   d.

   e.

   f.

B. Understanding the "How" of Visitation

1. The Do's of Visitation

   a.

   b.

   c.

   d.

   e.

   f.

g.

2. The Don'ts of Visitation

a.

b.

c.

d.

e.

3. When to Visit

a.

b.

c.

d.

e.

LESSON IV

ESTABLISHING A BIBLICAL RELATIONSHIP WITH THE PASTOR

One of the most talked about persons in the Christian community is the preacher. Negative talk and reports about crooked preachers have given the world an equally negative view of preachers as a whole. Tragically, the world will focus on a few preachers who are known to be less honest and will judge all preachers by those few. In the church, a large number of board members can be characterized as preacher-haters and fighters. The deacons often become the ones who feel it is their duty to watch the preachers. A preacher that has been called to a church, often arrives as a man under suspicion. Deacons, who are charged to be spiritual assistants, consequently become unified against the preacher. In frustration, the preacher may attempt to change things in his favor. However, hostile relationships ultimately become the final result.

The deacon must be careful to use his influence for the glory of God and not for the promotion of self-interest. Deacons who embrace the pastor's vision can help the congregation see where the pastor is going. When the congregation sees the pastor and deacons working together, this creates the climate needed to promote growth and harmony.

STEPS TO A BIBLICAL RELATIONSHIP WITH YOUR PASTOR

A. Place yourself in the Pastor's shoes.

B. Pray with and for your Pastor.

C. Affirm your Pastor.

D. Support your Pastor.

AN EFFECTIVE DEACON'S MINISTRY

I. Partnership with the Pew

II. Living Under the Lordship of Christ

III. Commitment to the Church

IV. Planning for an Effective Ministry

HOW TO S.E.R.V.E. IN TEAM MINISTRY

TEAM MINISTRY

A good sign of team ministry in action is evident in Acts 6:5-7. The first sign is the acceptance of the plan of action by the membership. When a plan for ministry is presented to the whole congregation, the members will delight in the effort. The plan allows the church to continue its growth mode, the preachers to preach and the church helpers to help.

The congregation selects persons to ensure the security of the ministry. The persons selected are individuals that the congregation respects. The issue is not so much about male or female servants--it is about willing and faithful persons doing the necessary things to produce a "happy" church. Selecting church helpers is no easy task. Things to consider are personality, character and spirituality. People who feel the "desire" to be a deacon or deaconess should rarely be considered.

The servants of Christ selected for church help accept the task given to them. There is no room for lazy persons in servant ministry. It should be understood that there is work to be done. Serving with a poor attitude will not help the church. The positive attitude of the servant of Christ accepts the task. The servant of Christ uses the gifts and talents they have to serve others. Those who selected the candidate will appreciate daily spiritual growth and duty. The church should not regret their selection. They should have the assurance that the deacon and deaconess will serve with a smile.

A. Principle of Team Ministry (Ecclesiastes 4:9-13)

_____
_____
_____
_____
_____

B. Purpose of Team Ministry (Ephesians 4:11-12)

_____
_____
_____
_____
_____

C. Preparation for Team Ministry (Luke 6:12)

_____
_____
_____
_____
_____

> *When the best leader's work is done,*
> *the people say, "We did it ourselves."*
> LAO-TSU
>
> • • • • • • •
>
> *No matter what accomplishments you make,*
> *somebody helps you.*
> ALTHEA GIBSON

Togetherness

Empowerment

Accountability

Mentoring

TEAM

A team is a group of people bound together by a commitment
to reach a shared goal.

Togetherness:_____

_____

_____

_____

_____

Empowerment:_____

_____

_____

_____

Accountability:_____

_____

_____

_____

Mentoring:_____

_____

_____

_____

A SAMPLE EXAM

1. How do you know that you are a Christian?
2. What is the Church?
3. What Scripture explains the Church's foundation?
4. Who is the head of the Church?
5. What Scripture gives us the great commission?
6. What are the three forms of church government?
7. What type of government is in the Baptist Church?
8. What are the methods in which one can join the Baptist Church?
9. What are the methods of dismissal from the Baptist Church?
10. How many ordinances are in the Baptist Church?
11. What is baptism?
12. What is the prerequisite for baptism?
13. Does baptism save a person?
14. What are the prerequisites for communion?
15. If baptism isn't essential to salvation, why do we practice it?
16. What is the meaning of the Lord's Supper?
17. What document of reference do Baptists affirm as the doctrinal teachings of Scripture?
18. What agreement should every Baptist adhere to as a member of a local congregation?
19. How many Scriptural offices are in the Baptist Church?
20. Who is the pastor?
21. Why was the office of the deacon originally established?

22. Is the office of the deacon by calling or appointment?

23. What does the word deacon mean?

24. What are some of the primary functions of the deacon?

25. What are the qualifications of a deacon and where are they found in Scripture?

26. Do you believe a deacon should be appointed for life and why?

27. If one is ordained as a deacon, is he a deacon in all Baptist Churches?

28. How should a deacon rule his own house?

29. List three things the deacon can do to assist the pastor?

30. Should a deacon tell his wife what is discussed in meetings with the pastor?

31. How many tables are there in the Baptist Church?

32. How should the ministries of the church be supported?

33. What should the deacon's attitude be about stewardship?

34. How many books are in the Bible?

35. What is the purpose of Holy Scriptures?

36. Where are the Ten Commandments, the Beatitudes and the Model Prayer found in the Holy Scriptures?

37. How are differences and disputes handled between members of the church?

38. What Scriptures tell what a person must do to be saved?

39. Who is Jesus?

40. Should deacons attend Sunday school, Bible Class, Prayer meeting?

CASE STUDY

Rev. Mack is the pastor of Truth Baptist Church, Anytown, North Carolina. The event is a conflict between Rev. Mack and Deacon Brown, in a board meeting. Rev. Mack had recently been called to serve as senior pastor of the Truth Baptist Church.

The Truth Baptist Church is forty-four years old. Rev. Mack is succeeding a pastor of thirty years by the name of Rev. Smith. Rev. Smith died, from a terminal illness, two and a half years before Rev. Mack's call. During the decline of Rev. Smith's health, the board of deacons controlled the church. Two associate ministers were also trying to use political maneuvers to become the pastor of the church. Rev. Mack is a strong-willed pastor, often straight forward, and did not mind confrontation. Deacon Brown was placed on the Deacon Board under the pastorate of Rev. Smith. He is the educated one on the Deacon Board. Although he was not the chairman of the deacons, others looked to him for answers. Deacon Brown had been a member of the Truth Baptist Church all of his life, along with other Committee members, and previously taught Bible Study under Rev. Smith's ministry. Rev. Mack had reviewed the finances, membership roll and overall ministry of the church. He noticed that the deacons did not tithe, and controlled every ministry of the church. He periodically heard from members that Deacon Brown, on more than one occasion, had taught against tithing in Bible Study and brought reference to the pastor's salary, saying, "We are paying him too much."

At the first deacon board meeting, Rev. Mack was called to open the meeting. He expressed to the deacons that they would preach and teach and emphasize tithing from the pulpit, and that it was necessary for all deacons to tithe. Deacon Brown immediately responded by saying, "I have a problem with that because tithing is an Old Testament principle." In addition to that, he did not want any of the members to feel intimidated because they were not tithing. Rev. Mack stated to Deacon Brown that he was wrong in Scripture and that his concerns were not for the people but for himself. The rest of the deacon board was beginning to join forces with Deacon Brown against newly elected Rev. Mack. The discussion became so heated that Rev. Mack adjourned the meeting.

About one week later, Rev. Mack attempted to have another deacon board meeting. Deacon Brown had greatly influenced other members of the board of deacons not to agree with anything Rev. Mack was presenting. Rev. Mack opened the meeting with a brief devotion and presented his agenda to the board of deacons for the upcoming church conference. Deacon Brown questioned almost every item on the agenda, and gave his usual negative responses. Rev. Mack recognized progress was not being made; therefore, he informed the board of deacons that if they could not work constructively, he would meet with the congregation to resolve the conflict.

Soon thereafter, a church meeting was held. Rev. Mack stated to the congregation that the deacons were not working with him and the deacons did not agree with the recommendations he was making.

QUESTIONS TO BE CONSIDERED

1. How will the church respond?

2. What actions would you take to resolve the conflict?

3. What are the issues in the case?

4. What are the biblical suggestions for resolutions?

5. What should be the role of the deacons in this case?

6. What would you say to Deacon Brown?

7. What would you say to Rev. Smith?

8. What would you say to the church?

CASE STUDY APPROACH OUTLINE

LEVEL I

DESCRIPTION OF THE EVENT

CRITICAL PROBLEM

BACKGROUND

LEVEL II

THEOLOGICAL REFLECTION

EXAMINE THE ISSUES

APPLICATION TO THE ISSUES

LEVEL III

CONCLUSION

JUDGE YOUR ACTIONS

EVALUATE YOUR ACTIONS

FUTURE APPLICATION

ENDNOTES

1. Trent C. Butler, Ph.D., *Holman Bible Dictionary* (Nashville: Holman Bible Publishers, 1994), pp. 344-345.

2. C. Gene Wilkes, *Jesus on Leadership* (Nashville: LifeWay Press, 1986), p. 11.

3. T. Dewitt Smith, *The Deacon in the Black Baptist Church* (U.S.A.: Church/Town Productions, 1983), p. 22.

4. Wayne Goodwin: Lecture Notes, "Paradigms on Leadership," Doctor of Ministry Program, Gordon-Conwell, Charlotte, NC, 1996, p. 23.

5. Augustine Confessions, *Book Seven--A.D. 397* (Kansas City: Sheed & Ward, 1943), chap. 21.

6. Robert Naylor, *The Work of the Deacon* (Nashville: Judson Press), p. 78.

7. Hiscoy, Edward T., *The Star Book for Ministers* (Valley Forge, Pa.: Judson Press, 1984), p. 219.

8. Ibid., p. 220.

9. C. E. Matthews, *Every Christian's Job* (Nashville: Convention Press, 1980), p. 8.

CPSIA information can be obtained
at www.ICGtesting.com
Printed in the USA
BVOW04s0325301017

499010BV00001B/9/P